A
Special Gift
for a
Special Friend

Presented to:

Laurie

From:

Linda

Date:

5 - 2 - 01

*The very best friends are the ones
who simply inspire us to be more like Jesus.*
— TWILA PARIS

I dedicate this book to
my best friend, wife, and
beautiful mother of my children,

Kristen Leigh Myers.

*Y*ou believed in me when I could not,
possessed hope when I did not,
and trusted God to work for the good
when I would not.

*M*ay God continue to use you
to apply His embrace on family, friends,
and fellow followers in the faith.

*Y*ours is a friendship worth celebrating.

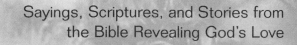
Sayings, Scriptures, and Stories from
the Bible Revealing God's Love

hugs
from
Heaven™

Celebrating
Friendship

G. A. Myers

HOWARD
PUBLISHING CO.

Our purpose at Howard Publishing is to:

- *Increase faith* in the hearts of growing Christians
- *Inspire holiness* in the lives of believers
- *Instill hope* in the hearts of struggling people everywhere

Because He's coming again!

Published by Howard Publishing Co., Inc.,
3117 North 7th Street, West Monroe, LA 71291-2227

01 02 03 04 05 06 07 08 09   10 9 8 7 6 5 4 3 2

Paraphrased Scriptures by LeAnn Weiss, owner of Encouragement Company,
3006 Brandywine Dr., Orlando, FL 32806

Edited by Philis Boultinghouse
Interior design by Stephanie Denney

Library of Congress Cataloging-in-Publication Data
Myers, G. A., 1955–
   Hugs from heaven : celebrating friendship : sayings, scriptures, and stories from the
  Bible revealing God's love / G.A. Myers ; personalized scriptures by LeAnn Weiss.
     p. cm.
   ISBN 1-58229-130-6
   1. Friendship—Religious aspects—Christianity. I. Weiss, LeAnn. II. Title.

BV4647.F7 M94 2000
241'.6762—dc21

                                     00-057497

Contents

Introduction

The *Hugs from Heaven* series is written with one purpose in mind: to make God's love more real and refreshing. This book is divided into topical sections consisting of a paraphrased, personalized scripture, an inspirational message, a poignant saying, a fictional story based on a particular passage of Scripture, and the actual account of the story from Scripture. Even though the narrative is fictional and the writer takes a creative course with the story, the biblical truths are uncompromised. Favorite Bible stories take on new meaning as you are transported to the scene to explore the thoughts and feelings of the people who were touched by heaven's embrace through the gift of friendship. May the message in this book and all the *Hugs from Heaven* books bring honor to God and praise to our Savior, Jesus Christ.

Chapter One

The Healing Touch of Friendship

I don't despise or reject you when you suffer. Instead, I tenderly listen to your cries for help. I comfort you when you're brokenhearted and save you when you're crushed in spirit. When you draw close to Me, I'll draw so close to you.

Compassionately,

Jesus

—from Psalms 22:24; 34:18; James 4:8

Inspirational
Message

Would you describe yourself as a healer? Probably not, but that would be a great mistake. I know that your idea of a healer might be a skilled surgeon working to save a life with scalpel in hand and a crack team of nurses gathered around. Maybe it's the family physician carefully listening to an ailing heart with a stethoscope and trained ears or looking at x-rays against the light with attentive eyes. Now you can add one more picture to the healing heroes in your mind. Yours!

Oh, you may never cut away some life-threatening cancer with a scalpel, but your friendship removes the heartache of loneliness. A warm embrace or tender touch from you is like a refreshing rain that washes through your friends and brings renewal. You may never listen through a stethoscope or scan x-rays, but your ears are attentive, listening carefully to your friends' concerns. And it seems that your eyes have been trained to see into the slumping soul and brittle spirit that needs encouraging and strengthening.

Yes, your touch, eyes, and ears are tools for healing, and you use them as skillfully as any surgeon or physician ever could. If you ever wonder how your friendship affects others, if you ever ask yourself whether your friendship is needed, remember the great physician who healed hearts, bodies, and lives without a single medical instrument. The power of His presence and His love was enough to make the unhealthy person whole.

You resemble Him.

If you have a wounded heart—

and all of us do to some extent or another—

know that Jesus has positioned himself as your friend.

—WAYNE WATSON

Believing
the
Impossible

It was midafternoon, and Hannah felt the strength-sapping heat of the sun even more keenly than the other expectant people who lined the streets of Capernaum. A severely thin wrist appeared from under her cloak and ran across her gaunt face to wipe the beads of perspiration that had formed across her dark brow and petite nose. It was easy to see that at one time she had been radiantly attractive. However, high cheekbones and strikingly deep blue eyes were all that remained of her swiftly escaping beauty.

Twelve years earlier, Hannah had been a much-loved young girl with high hopes. And in this small community of Capernaum, her friends and family had even higher expectations. Everyone, including Hannah herself, was sure that she would marry well and have exceptionally beautiful children like herself. She lived what some had called a charmed life. All who knew her believed that God had personally touched her with His blessings. But something happened in her eighteenth year of life that no one could have predicted and, it seemed, no one was prepared for.

It began one afternoon while Hannah was helping her mother prepare for the evening meal. A knife slipped and sliced across her index finger. The bleeding was excessive, and all attempts to stop the flow were totally ineffective. It was not until several hours later that her mother finally began to see the blood clot and cease its relentless stream. The whole experience left her mother and father fearful. Not just for her health, but for what the community would think if they found out. No one would want anything to do with a young woman subject to bleeding. They watched her closely that night as she lay in her bed, shivering, pale, and weak from blood loss.

It happened again one day when she was with her friends and cut her foot on a sharp rock. The friends panicked because they couldn't stop the bleeding, and the news of Hannah's problem soon spread through the community like a cold wind. Icy stares and receptions greeted Hannah on the streets. One by one her friends deserted her, and there were absolutely no suitors to consider for marriage, because no one wanted anything to do with a young woman who was subject to bleeding.

Over the next few years, she depleted her family's money, desperately going from physician to physician—each one promising a cure, each one claiming to have the knowledge to supply the healing she so hungered for, each one eagerly taking her money. She anxiously took their medicines and followed their instructions, but her continued bouts with bleeding took away her hope, leaving her weakened, helpless, and heartbroken. By her thirtieth birthday, she had stopped searching for cures and had surrendered to the forced exile placed on her by former friends and neighbors. There was no place in their hearts for a woman subject to bleeding, so she took a small dwelling on the outskirts of town and lived alone, waiting to die. That is, until now.

For the past several days, her parents had been telling her about a man named Jesus. He was a true friend of the hurting, they said. In fact, they said, "He is a true friend to anyone who comes to Him." They had heard Him speak on a mount just north of Capernaum, and His teaching was like pure water cascading into the hearts of all those who were there. "But that was just the beginning," her mother told her. "As Jesus walked down from the mountainside, a man with leprosy appeared. Everyone started backing away when they saw the leper come and kneel before Jesus."

"Did Jesus push him away?" Hannah eagerly asked.

"No, Hannah. He reached out His hand and touched the man and said, 'Be clean.'"

"What happened next?" Hannah's voice and expression wore the excitement of youthful curiosity for the first time in years.

Her mother almost whispered, "The leper was healed."

Hannah raised her spindly fingers to her lips and gasped as if she had just discovered a hidden treasure. And as far as she was concerned, she had. Hannah kept saying to herself, "He touched a leper. I can't believe He touched a leper." The healing hadn't escaped her notice, but she was stunned by the willingness of this man to befriend the outcast, the unclean, and the forgotten, because that is what she had become.

Quickly, she gathered her things, along with a cloak to keep herself hidden from the crowds, and said to her mother and father, "I must go see Jesus. I just know that if I can see Him and touch Him, I will be healed." She had run through her doorway, waving to her parents, as if she were a child again. She now found herself in a sea of people baking in the hot sun and waiting for Jesus to come into Capernaum.

The minute Jesus appeared in the street, He was totally surrounded by the swarming crowd. Hannah caught just a glimpse of Him before the crowd bumped her and pushed her away. She had no strength to fight through this throng of people to get to Jesus, but she knew that somehow, she must! *Hannah,* she said sternly to herself, *you can do this.* Gathering every ounce of strength she could muster, she began to work her way through the crowd. She prayed that no one would recognize her, for if anyone did, she would be chased out of town.

Finally, out of breath and with little strength remaining, she found herself within a few feet of Jesus. She could see His smiling face through the sea of flailing arms. She came up behind Him in the crowd and reached out to touch His cloak, thinking, *If I can just touch His clothes, I will be healed.* Straining, stretching, the tip of her fingers finally made contact with a fold of His cloak. Instantly, she felt a strangely refreshing sensation rush through her entire body, as if she had been drenched by a wave in the sea. Immediately her bleeding stopped, and she felt in her body that she was freed from her suffering.

In the same instant, Jesus realized that power had gone out from Him. Whirling around, He asked, "Who touched My clothes?"

"You see the people crowding against You," His disciples answered, "and yet You ask, 'Who touched Me?'" But Jesus kept looking around to see who had done it.

Then Hannah, knowing what had happened to her, came and fell at His feet and, trembling with fear, told Him the whole truth. Jesus lifted Hannah to her feet and brushed away the tears that were pouring down her face. She hadn't felt the touch of a friend or anyone else in so long that her knees almost buckled from joy.

Jesus looked into her eyes, placed His arm around her,

and gently said, "Daughter, your faith has healed you. Go in peace and be freed from your suffering."

As Jesus walked away, He kept His smiling eyes fastened on hers until He was interrupted by a group of men wanting to speak with Him. Hannah framed those eyes in her mind and pledged never to forget them. The crowd moved past her and left her standing alone. Then Hannah turned and ran home to her parents and told them everything that had happened. She never went back to the little dwelling on the outskirts of town, and from that day on, she became the best friend of all those who were weak, helpless, and heartbroken.

Scriptural Account

A large crowd followed and pressed around him. And a woman was there who had been subject to bleeding for twelve years. She had suffered a great deal under the care of many doctors and had spent all she had, yet instead of getting better she grew worse. When she heard about Jesus, she came up behind him in the crowd and touched his cloak, because she thought, "If I just touch his clothes, I will be healed." Immediately her bleeding stopped and she felt in her body that she was freed from her suffering.

At once Jesus realized that power had gone out from him. He turned around in the crowd and asked, "Who touched my clothes?"

"You see the people crowding against you," his disciples answered, "and yet you can ask, 'Who touched me?'"

But Jesus kept looking around to see who had done it. Then the woman, knowing what had happened to her, came and fell at his feet and, trembling with fear, told him the whole truth. He said to her, "Daughter, your faith has healed you. Go in peace and be freed from your suffering."

—Mark 5:24b–34

Reflections on the healing touch of friendship in my life...

_____

_____

_____

_____

_____

_____

_____

_____

_____

_____

_____

_____

_____

_____

_____

_____

_____

_____

My intercessor is my friend...he pleads with God as a man pleads for his friend.

—Job 16:20–21

Chapter Two

The Assurance of Friendship

My hope won't disappoint you because I've poured out My love into your heart by the Holy Spirit. I'm faithful to all of My promises to you. Because of My great love for you, you are not consumed. My compassions for you never fail and are new every morning. I mean it when I promise never to desert or forsake you.

With you always to the very end,

Your Faithful God

—from Romans 5:5; Psalm 145:13;
Lamentations 3:22–23; Deuteronomy 31:6

Inspirational
Message
⁓⧫⁓

$\mathscr{G}$et ready for a very nice compliment you will most certainly want to hear. It may come as a shock to you, but to those who know you best, it is an accepted fact. No, it's not about your youthful good looks or irresistible charm. It is something even better, and it fits you just right. The compliment is that you are a good friend who is always there and you have some very good friends who love you and need you.

Oh, you probably don't think about it much, but others do. For you bring caring, comfort, courage, and assurance into the lives of your friends.

Isn't that the true blessing of friendship? When the cold wind of doubt sweeps through a heart, it is a friend like you who brings a warm embrace that ignites within the soul a fire of cozy confidence. If the future of a friend begins to look bleak, there you are cheering her on with encouraging words and an unrelenting faith. You shed fresh tears with those who hurt, celebrate with those who receive good news, pick up those who fall down, and quietly listen to those who are aching to be heard.

Yes, that's you at the birthday party serving others and saving the day. There you are, sitting with kids, stopping by the store, and standing by. You are there at giddy graduations, ghastly recitals, and grim grave sites. Quite simply, you are like one who greeted friends at an empty tomb with the words "Do not be afraid," and gave them the assurance that friendship is forever.

My, how that compliment looks good on you.

When we preach the resurrection of Christ,

we are preaching the miracle of love.

When we preach the return of Christ,

we are preaching the fulfillment of love.

—BILLY GRAHAM

Do Not
Be
Afraid

As the first light of day crept across the room, it discovered two figures kneeling on the floor, side by side, arms draped across each other's shoulders, praying. When one woman would falter and begin to weep, the other would take up the prayer until she could no longer go on.

Over the last couple of years, these two women had shared more than most friends share in a lifetime. They had shared aspirations and dreams, causes and concerns, fights and failures. They had walked the same paths, eaten the same meals, slept under the same stars, and above all, followed the same man—a man they believed in; a man they had seen heal the lame, blind, and broken, and even raise the dead; a man they had watched suffer and die just the past Friday evening. Now, on Sunday morning they shared their common grief.

They were two of the most unlikely friends in the world. Everyone who knew them commented on the irony of their shared name, because their similarities stopped there. Mary the mother of James was short, stout, silver-haired, and soft-spoken. Her kind eyes, fixed smile, and sweet disposition made her a beacon of light to friends and strangers alike. If neighbors, friends, or family experienced joy or tragedy, success or failure, hopefulness or heartbreak, Mary was the first to know. She was the consummate encourager and could always be trusted with a confidence or confession.

Mary Magdalene, on the other hand, had once been possessed by seven demons. Jesus had driven them out of her, and Mary had followed him ever since. She was tall, slim, with coal black hair that hung all the way down past her waist. Her features were sharp and chiseled. Although her expression had softened some since her liberation, a stubborn hardness remained. Mary possessed an inexhaustible enthusiasm and outspokenness that some found threatening but the other Mary found wonderfully refreshing.

They had become immediate friends when, after the exorcism, Jesus arranged for the other Mary to come and minister to her. Mary Magdalene talked for hours to the other Mary about the horrors of the possession and how it had affected her. The other Mary had listened unwaveringly and watched intently as tears washed away years of pain and suffering. From that night on, they were the best of friends, growing in their faith and devoting themselves to helping others.

But their faith was not strong now. They spoke with uncertainty, prayed in desperation, and wondered what would happen since the center of their lives had been murdered.

After watching Joseph of Arimathea close the grave of Jesus on Friday evening by rolling a large stone in front of the tomb, they had committed to come back together on Sunday. They felt that just being near the body of Jesus might soothe the immense pain they felt at the loss of the One they loved so very much. So on this early Sunday morning, they rose from their prayers, gathered the spices they hoped to place on Jesus' body, closed the door to Mary Magdalene's house, and hesitantly started for the grave site.

The two Marys walked hand in hand and inhaled deeply the fresh sweetness left in the air by an early morning rainfall. They attempted to sing some of the songs of worship that Jesus had taught them, but with every familiar verse, they pictured Jesus moving His arms to the beat of the song, encouraging the disciples to pick up the tune, and they would dissolve into tears.

The two women had to stop several times and bolster each other's courage to face the sealed tomb. They thought their dreams lay dead in that tomb. They believed their journey had ended. They wondered what they would do now. Little did they know that their friendship, faith, and future were about to be reignited, lit by the friend they thought they had lost.

With the tomb not one hundred yards away, the earth suddenly began to shake violently. It knocked both Marys to the ground. They held each other tightly until the tremors ceased. They looked at each other and asked simultaneously, "What was that?"

Trembling and shaken, they began walking quickly toward the tomb. When they arrived, they were startled by the scene before them. The stone had been rolled away, and an angel of God sat upon it. The guards who had been watching the tomb lay as motionless as dead men. Both Marys gasped, covered their mouths with their hands, and dropped the spices they were carrying.

The angel said to the women, "Do not be afraid, for I know that you are looking for Jesus, who was crucified. He is not here; He has risen, just as He said." He moved behind them and placed his arms around their shoulders. "Come and see the place where He lay. Then go quickly and tell His disciples: 'He has risen from the dead and is going ahead of you into Galilee. There you will see Him.' Now I have told you."

When the women finally realized it was true—that their beloved Jesus was not dead but alive—they embraced each other and began to weep with joy. They then turned, arm in arm, and hurried away from the tomb and toward Galilee.

Suddenly, just a few yards from the tomb, Jesus stood before them. Smiling warmly, He said, "Greetings." The two Marys came to Him, clasped His feet, and worshiped Him.

Then Jesus said to them, "Do not be afraid. Go and tell my brothers to go to Galilee; there they will see Me."

As the two women, now full of joy, skipped and danced toward the city, they sang their favorite song Jesus had taught them. Their friendship had tasted the bitterness of loss and the sweetness of resurrection. They were assured in their hearts that their friendship would last a lifetime, and now, well beyond.

Scriptural Account

After the Sabbath, at dawn on the first day of the week, Mary Magdalene and the other Mary went to look at the tomb.

There was a violent earthquake, for an angel of the Lord came down from heaven and, going to the tomb, rolled back the stone and sat on it. His appearance was like lightning, and his clothes were white as snow. The guards were so afraid of him that they shook and became like dead men.

The angel said to the women, "Do not be afraid, for I know that you are looking for Jesus, who was crucified. He is not here; he has risen, just as he said. Come and see the place where he lay. Then go quickly and tell his disciples: 'He has risen from the dead and is going ahead of you into Galilee. There you will see him.' Now I have told you."

So the women hurried away from the tomb, afraid yet filled with joy, and ran to tell his disciples. Suddenly Jesus met them. "Greetings," he said. They came to him, clasped his feet and worshiped him. Then Jesus said to them, "Do not be afraid. Go and tell my brothers to go to Galilee; there they will see me."

—Matthew 28:1–10

Reflections on the assurances friendship has brought to my life...

_____

_____

_____

_____

_____

_____

_____

_____

_____

_____

_____

_____

_____

Perfume and incense bring joy to the heart, and the pleasantness of one's friend springs from his earnest counsel.

—Proverbs 27:9

If one falls down, his friend can help him up.

—Ecclesiastes 4:10

Chapter Three

The
Power
of
Friendship

My friend, nothing can separate you from My love. Even in times of trouble or hardship or persecution or lack, you are always more than a conqueror through My love which supersedes anything in your past, present, or future. Not even death can stop My unconditional love for you.

Love Always,

Your King and Friend

—from Romans 8:35–39

Inspirational
Message

$\mathcal{T}$he attraction to Jesus was compelling. But what was it that made thousands want to be close to Him? What was it that changed everyone who engaged the friendship of Jesus? We know that it wasn't His looks that attracted others. We are told that He was a common looking person. He might have looked like you or like me. In fact, he probably wanted us to see ourselves in Him.

Certainly His appeal had something to do with the words He spoke. They were kind even to those who were not, they were forgiving to those who did not deserve it, and they were tender to the frailest of hearts.

And surely people were drawn to His inviting touch. His arms were always extended to the children, the heartbroken, the sick, and the mistreated. It's easy even now to see His busy hands warmly grasping the arms of new friends, placing the head of a weeping follower on His shoulder, or touching the cheek of a lost soul looking for life.

And of course, one of the things that made friendship with Jesus so irresistible was His warm and wonderful promises: The promise of a new life no matter how a person had misused the old one. The promise of never being hungry, thirsty, lost, or lonely. The promise that life is never over, even though it may seem so to the rest of the world.

Whatever it was that drew crowds to Christ, it changed forever those He befriended.

Even though you may never be followed by thousands of followers, you will have a great impact on your friends as you follow Christ. Simply let your words express love, your touch be inviting, and your promises always true. Even though your friendships may not be written down for history, those whom you befriend will say they were never the same after they called you friend.

You are…infinitely dear to the Father,

unspeakably precious to Him.

You are never, not for one second, alone.

—NORMA DOWTY

An
Unwanted Visitor
and a
Welcome Friend

The brilliance of the white sun on the Bethany landscape contrasted sharply with the mood of its citizenry. The normally bustling pace of its people had come to a startling halt. An unwelcome visitor had come to town. His cold shadow and frigid fingers had touched every individual within the town's borders. Even after he left, his hot breath served as a stinging reminder that he would return. The visitor was death.

In this instance, his numbing effect was intensified by his choice of victim. It seemed as though no one in this community, which served as the gateway to Jerusalem, was untouched by the deceased, Lazarus, or by his sisters, Mary and Martha. This beloved family had become well known as a friend to all in Bethany. Their concern for the hurting, hospitality to the hungry, kindness to the rejected, and benevolence to anyone who had need was legendary—not only in Bethany but all the way to Jerusalem.

Even four days after Lazarus was laid to rest in the tomb, many from Jerusalem remained in Bethany to comfort Martha and Mary in the loss of their brother. However, even in this time of great heartache, it was the sisters of Lazarus who did most of the comforting—and there were many to comfort, for everyone grieved the death of the man who had somehow become friend to so many. The man who had become a fixture of fondness with his busy and affectionate hands, tall frame, long gait, and perpetually bright smile was gone. The pain of loss could be measured in the longing eyes, expressionless faces, silenced tongues, and tear-stained cheeks of those in Bethany.

There had been a time, however, when Bethany would not have mourned the death of Lazarus or bothered to mourn with his sisters. Indeed, the community might have even quietly cheered the demise of the likes of Lazarus. For in the not too distant past, the reputation of Lazarus and his sisters was the subject of venomous gossip on the street corners and cruel whispers at the market. Lazarus had been described by most who knew him as distant, self-serving, prideful, and mean. The townspeople knew to keep their distance when Lazarus walked down the street. Mary was infamous for her rebellious spirit and brutally honest tongue. Martha was regarded as a hermit who rarely appeared in public, and when she did, she said nothing to anyone. Many speculated that she had an evil spirit or was a mental cripple.

But on a visit to Jerusalem for a religious feast, something remarkable had happened. On the last day of the Feast of Tabernacles, Lazarus and Martha were standing in the temple courts when they heard a man speaking. He was saying things the two of them had never heard before, and His words cracked the brittle shell that had formed around their hearts. Lazarus and Martha asked those around them who the man was. They said His name was Jesus. Some of them whispered that He was a prophet; others said He was evil. Lazarus and Martha just wanted to hear more.

Finally, Jesus stood up and said, "If a man is thirsty, let

him come to Me and drink. Whoever believes in Me, as the Scripture has said, streams of water will flow from within him." This caused quite a stir in the crowd, but it caused a raging storm of emotion in Lazarus and Martha. They came to Jesus and said, "We are thirsty; we want to hear more, teacher." Jesus answered, "Then you shall, My friends, come follow Me."

The next day Jesus appeared again in the temple court, and a crowd gathered, including Lazarus, Martha, and now Mary. As He was teaching, a half-naked woman was hurled down at His feet. A group of religious leaders had set her up with the husband of a woman in town so they could catch her and test Jesus on how He would judge her. Mary's eyes flashed with anger as they told Jesus they had caught her in the act of adultery and that Moses would have her put to death.

Fear gripped Mary, Lazarus, and Martha as the group of men began to pick up stones to throw at the woman. But Jesus bent down next to the accused, looked at her with an assuring expression, and began to write something on the ground. When He straightened, He said to the accusers: "If any one of you is without sin, let him begin stoning her."

Martha closed her eyes, expecting the worst. Then she

began to hear the dull thud of stones dropping harmlessly to the ground. The accusers walked away, and Jesus stood alone with the prostitute. Mary didn't hear the entire exchange, but she did hear Him say, "Then neither do I condemn you, go now and leave your life of sin."

As the woman walked away, a stunned Mary felt a softening in her own heart and was drawn to the massive mercy of this unusual man who dared challenge the false justice of these hypocritical men.

After spending a few more days with Jesus; Lazarus, Martha, and Mary returned to Bethany with beaming smiles, sparkling eyes, and transformed hearts. Everyone wanted to know what had brought such a stunning change. Over and over again, they told the story of their new friendship with a man who had touched them as no one ever had. As they told the story, the three offered the kind of friendship they had found in Jesus, and the love for Lazarus, Mary, and Martha blossomed throughout Bethany.

Then, within the last couple of weeks, neighbors began to notice a slowing in Lazarus's gait. His color turned pale, his breathing became labored, and though he never stopped smiling, pain seeped into his expression from time to time.

He had collapsed a week ago and had told Mary and Martha that he felt the life draining from him. Word was sent to Jesus. Surely He would want to come and heal His friend the way He had healed so many others. But He tarried, and when He finally arrived, it was too late. The unwelcome visitor had arrived first, and his visit left an occupied tomb and empty hearts.

Suddenly a stir began among the crowd. Jesus had arrived. Martha had gone out to meet Him, then He sent for Mary. Mary fell at Jesus' feet, saying, "Lord, if You had been here, my brother would not have died."

When Jesus saw her weeping, along with all those who had come out with her, He was deeply moved and troubled. And then Jesus wept. At this display of emotion, several in the crowd remarked how much Jesus must have loved Lazarus.

Jesus, again deeply moved, came to the tomb with an expression that had changed from sorrow to confrontation, and He spoke firmly, saying, "Take away the stone." Martha reminded Jesus that by this time the body would smell. Jesus placed His hands on her shoulders and said, "Did I not tell you that if you believed, you would see the glory of God?" After lifting His eyes toward heaven and saying a short prayer, Jesus faced the tomb. With a thundering voice, He exclaimed, "Lazarus, come out!"

Inside the tomb, eyes opened, a heart resumed its rhythmic beat, and the strength of life filled a dead body. When Lazarus appeared at the mouth of the tomb, a stunned crowd watched in utter silence. Jesus smiled at Lazarus and said, "Take off the grave clothes and let him go." Mary and Martha, along with several others, rushed to Lazarus, tore the wrappings from him, and smothered him with embracing arms.

The hands that had been covered in the cloth of the dead became active and affectionate once again. The legs and feet that were wrapped for burial resumed their welcomed, long strides. A face once covered for the sleep of death now beamed a bright smile, reflecting the heart of a town whose best friend had just returned.

Above all, the power of friendship in the visitor named Jesus proved greater than the power of the destruction in the visitor called death.

Scriptural Account

The teachers of the law and the Pharisees brought in a woman caught in adultery. They made her stand before the group and said to Jesus, "Teacher, this woman was caught in the act of adultery. In the Law Moses commanded us to stone such women. Now what do you say?" They were using this question as a trap, in order to have a basis for accusing him.

But Jesus bent down and started to write on the ground with his finger. When they kept on questioning him, he straightened up and said to them, "If any one of you is without sin, let him be the first to throw a stone at her." Again he stooped down and wrote on the ground.

At this, those who heard began to go away one at a time, the older ones first, until only Jesus was left, with the woman still standing there. Jesus straightened up and asked her, "Woman, where are they? Has no one condemned you?"

"No one, sir," she said.

"Then neither do I condemn you," Jesus declared. "Go now and leave your life of sin."

Now a man named Lazarus was sick. He was from Bethany, the village of Mary and her sister Martha. This Mary, whose brother Lazarus now lay sick, was the same one who poured perfume on the Lord and wiped his feet with her hair. So the sisters sent word to Jesus, "Lord, the one you love is sick."

On his arrival, Jesus found that Lazarus had already been in the tomb for four days. Bethany was less than two miles from Jerusalem, and many Jews had come to Martha and Mary to comfort them in the loss of their brother. When Martha heard that Jesus was coming, she went out to meet him, but Mary stayed at home.

"Lord," Martha said to Jesus, "if you had been here, my brother would not have died. But I know that even now God will give you whatever you ask."

Jesus said to her, "Your brother will rise again."

Martha answered, "I know he will rise again in the resurrection at the last day."

Jesus said to her, "I am the resurrection and the life. He who believes in me will live, even though he dies; and whoever lives and believes in me will never die. Do you believe this?"

"Yes, Lord," she told him, "I believe that you are the Christ, the Son of God, who was to come into the world."

And after she had said this, she went back and called her sister Mary aside. "The Teacher is here," she said, "and is asking for you." When Mary heard this, she got up quickly and went to him.

When Mary reached the place where Jesus was and saw him, she fell at his feet and said, "Lord, if you had been here, my brother would not have died."

When Jesus saw her weeping, and the Jews who had come along with her also weeping, he was deeply moved in spirit and troubled. "Where have you laid him?" he asked.

"Come and see, Lord," they replied.

Jesus wept.

Then the Jews said, "See how he loved him!"

But some of them said, "Could not he who opened the eyes of the blind man have kept this man from dying?"

Jesus, once more deeply moved, came to the tomb. It was a cave with a stone laid across the entrance. "Take away the stone," he said.

"But, Lord," said Martha, the sister of the dead man, "by this time there is a bad odor, for he has been there four days."

Then Jesus said, "Did I not tell you that if you believed, you would see the glory of God?"

So they took away the stone. Then Jesus looked up and said, "Father, I thank you that you have heard me. I knew that you always hear me, but I said this for the benefit of the people standing here, that they may believe that you sent me."

When he had said this, Jesus called in a loud voice, "Lazarus, come out!" The dead man came out, his hands and feet wrapped with strips of linen, and a cloth around his face.

Jesus said to them, "Take off the grave clothes and let him go."

—John 8:3–11; 11:1–3, 17–29, 32–44

Reflections on how the power of friendship has impacted my life...

_____

_____

_____

_____

_____

_____

_____

_____

_____

_____

_____

_____

_____

_____

_____

_____

_____

_____

_____

_____

A man of many companions may come to ruin, but there is a friend who sticks closer than a brother.

—Proverbs 18:24

A friend loves at all times.

—Proverbs 17:17

Chapter Four

The Extravagance of Friendship

$\mathcal{I}$ am the source of every good and perfect gift. Because of My endless love for you, I even sacrificed My Son, Jesus, for you. You can trust Me to graciously give you all things! I am able to make all grace abound to you, so that in all things at all times, having all that you need, you will abound in every good work. I'll make you rich in every way so you can be generous on every occasion, directing your thanksgiving to Me.

Extravagantly,

Your Heavenly Father

—from James 1:17; Romans 8:32; 2 Corinthians 9:8, 11

Inspirational
Message

$\mathscr{I}$f you were asked to describe friendship, what would you say? You might use words like *loyalty, faithfulness, dedication,* or *devotion.* You might think of the characteristics of friendship, like sensitivity, sharing, understanding, or gentleness.

However, there is another way to describe friendship that reflects its beauty and blessings in perhaps a more adequate way. It may not be something that would simply pop into your mind, but if you think about it, you will probably agree. A proper description of friendship is "an extravagant gift." If you look up the word *extravagant* in the dictionary, you will find in its definition the phrase, "exceeding the bounds of reason." The word *gift* is defined as something given without any repayment expected. Now isn't that a perfect way to describe good friendship?

Examine the extravagant gifts of true friendship. Time is offered without counting seconds or minutes. When friends are called they come without glancing at their watches, calling time and temperature, or wondering when they will no longer be needed. Resources are offered without restriction. When friends are in need, there are no *whys, whats, wheres,* or *whens* exchanged. There is simply the sound of an opening purse, wallet, checkbook, or heart.

When friends hurt, compassion is felt and comfort offered. One cannot weep without the other tasting salt and wiping away tears. And what about the gifts exchanged? A friend will search with reckless abandon until the perfect present is found, fitted, or formed. In other words, self is sacrificed for the sake of someone else.

You have a friend who fits this description perfectly. He gave you the extravagant gift of His life. He saw the nails being placed in His hands and feet before it ever happened, and He never turned away. His friendship with you wouldn't let Him. He saw you as an extravagant gift worth having. He also knew that you would be a true friend to others.

Give for the joy of giving—

if you only "give to get" you are not giving,

you are trading.

—MARY C. CROWLEY

The
Extravagant
Gift

Mary brushed her thick, black, waist-length hair away from her face in an effort to persuade it not to distract her from her work. As her slender, well-worked fingers masterfully kneaded the dough that would soon become a tasty companion to an already delightful meal, she periodically wiped her hands across the heavily stained apron that wrapped around her thin waist. Her dark eyes—perched on her high, well-defined cheekbones—danced with excitement. She could hardly contain the elation she felt as the evening celebration drew nearer. She looked over at her sister, Martha, and smiled broadly as she said, "Won't it be wonderful to have so many of our friends with us tonight?" And with added emphasis she exclaimed, "Especially our honored guest, Jesus!"

The older, much heavier, and much more serious Martha returned an uneasy smile and said, "Yes, I just hope we have enough food for everyone."

Mary looked at what she felt was a rather excessive mound of food and raised her hand to her mouth to keep from laughing out loud at her sister's needless concern. "Martha," Mary chuckled, "we have enough food here to serve the whole Roman army."

Martha ran the back of her hand against the sides of her head, making sure that her hair was neatly pulled back and no rebellious strands of gray had escaped. She then sighed a sigh Mary had become all too familiar with and said, "It may look like enough to you, but when everyone arrives, it will go very quickly. You know how those fishermen eat. Why, Peter and his brother almost eat their weight in food every time they sit down to a meal. I just want everything to be perfect."

Mary reached out and reassuringly stroked Martha on the

back and said the words she had repeated a hundred times before, whenever Martha showed undue concern: "Dear sister, you are the greatest hostess the world has ever known. Your meals are near perfection, and there is always food to spare. Why, if I were going to invite a king to our home, I wouldn't think of asking anyone but you to handle the whole affair."

Even though Martha answered Mary's statement of confidence with a self-deprecating, "Well, I don't know about that," she always appreciated hearing Mary's encouraging words because she knew she really did mean them. Martha, it seemed, was always in need of reassurance, and the perceptive Mary was delighted to provide it.

While Mary waited for the dough to rise, she moved to the doorway that opened to the road that ran through the middle of Bethany. As she looked toward the east, she could see the swirling clouds of dust in the distance being raised by the mounting crowds headed toward Jerusalem. She imagined the countless sandaled feet, rolling wagon wheels, and animal hooves that were stirring the earth on the way to the Passover. She could practically hear the clutter of conversation between friends and family about everything from politics and power to parenting and marriage. The throng of worshipers were still a day away from converging on Mary's beloved Bethany, the town that served as the gateway to the Mount of Olives and Jerusalem. Mary herself would soon be among them, covering the day's walk to the holy city to celebrate the most wonderful of all holidays, the day when God spared His people with the blood of the lamb.

Turning her gaze to the west, Mary looked toward the peak of the hill that looked out over the holy city on the other side. In the distance she recognized the familiar silhouette of Jesus walking with His disciples toward Bethany. He was wiping the moisture from His forehead and speaking passionately to His disciples. Mary called out to Martha, "They're coming! Martha, they're coming down the road right now."

Mary heard Martha's muted voice, as she passed by the window, saying something about getting the bread baked, but Mary was already running toward the group of welcome friends. As she came closer to the group, Mary could tell by Jesus' expression that He was telling His friends something of great importance. Jesus' moist eyes met Mary's at the exact time she heard Him say, "As you know, the Passover is just days away, and the Son of Man will be handed over to be crucified."

The words hit her hard, making her feel as though someone had pushed her back on her heels. Some of those with Jesus shook their heads and whispered, "What is He saying; they won't try to hurt Him." She heard Peter declare, "Just let them try; we'll protect Him!" Jesus didn't move His eyes an inch; He just looked into Mary's eyes and nodded in a way that told her it would happen just as He said.

Mary felt herself almost stop breathing as she heard the first clap of thunder and looked behind Jesus at the storm clouds gathering over Jerusalem. Suddenly Jesus' teachings came rushing through her mind like a flash flood, and she remembered the words *Passover, Lamb of God, the blood of the Lamb, God spared His people.* Jesus was now standing before her, and He gathered her in His arms and embraced her; and with a whisper in her ear, He said, "You understand, don't you, Mary?"

Lazarus, whom Jesus had raised from the dead, came running up to the group from the house and exclaimed for all to hear, "Come, everyone, a dinner has been prepared in honor of Jesus. Martha has everything prepared; it is a feast you will certainly not forget."

With that, the disciples followed behind Lazarus to the house while Mary walked alongside Jesus in shocked silence.

As they reached the door, the others went in and reclined, but Mary stopped Jesus and with tears now flowing from her eyes, she asked, "Is there no other way?"

Jesus said nothing; He simply wiped the tears from Mary's cheek and joined His friends. Mary stood at the door a moment longer, looking up the road and examining the gathering storm. She then walked into the house and past a perturbed Martha, who was now serving their friends the meal.

Mary didn't even hear Martha as she chided her to help with the food. She went to the next room and directly to a large chest in the corner. She lifted the heavy lid and began looking for something hidden deep inside. When her hands grasped what she was looking for, a faint smile appeared on her face. As she lifted her hand, a beautiful alabaster jar appeared. She knelt down and lifted the jar and her voice toward heaven. "My God, You are my God, and the One You have sent is the Lamb. He is also my teacher, my hope, my strength, and my closest friend. This alabaster jar of perfume neither costs enough nor smells beautiful enough for what it is about to be used. It was intended for my wedding night, but now I use it to prepare a loved one for burial—the One You have sent. My heart breaks like this jar, but my soul is filled with the fragrance of hope."

Mary entered the room that was now filled with bustling conversation and laughter. She stood behind the silent Jesus, broke open the jar, and poured the pint of pure nard on His head. As the perfume moved down His hair and onto His shoulders, Jesus closed His eyes and breathed deeply so that the perfume filled His nostrils and lungs. Mary took some of the perfume and poured it on His feet. Knowing this would be one of the last times she would have Him with her, she ached for the holy moment to linger, like the aroma that now filled every space of the small home. To keep the anointing alive in her heart for as long as she could, she took her hair from around her back, over her shoulders, and held the thick strands in her hand. She then began to gently wipe His feet with her hair so that His fragrance would remain on her, with her, and in her memories for as long as she lived.

The room went quiet until the silence was broken by

Judas, who said, "Why wasn't this perfume sold and the money given to the poor? It was worth a year's wages."

"Leave her alone," Jesus replied. "It was meant that she should save this perfume for the day of My burial." As Mary arose, Jesus said, "You will always have the poor among you, but you will not always have Me." As Mary started to move away, Jesus arose and gave her another embrace and whispered to her once more, "This extravagant gift of friendship will never be forgotten."

Mary looked into His eyes and whispered back to Him, "Neither will the extravagant gift You are about to give."

Mary walked slowly toward the door, holding her hair close to her face. Standing outside, she watched the growing storm clouds gather over Jerusalem.

Scriptural Account

Six days before the Passover, Jesus arrived at Bethany, where Lazarus lived, whom Jesus had raised from the dead. Here a dinner was given in Jesus' honor. Martha served, while Lazarus was among those reclining at the table with him. Then Mary took about a pint of pure nard, an expensive perfume; she poured it on Jesus' feet and wiped his feet with her hair. And the house was filled with the fragrance of the perfume.

But one of his disciples, Judas Iscariot, who was later to betray him, objected, "Why wasn't this perfume sold and the money given to the poor? It was worth a year's wages." He did not say this because he cared about the poor but because he was a thief; as keeper of the money bag, he used to help himself to what was put into it.

"Leave her alone," Jesus replied. "It was intended that she should save this perfume for the day of my burial. You will always have the poor among you, but you will not always have me."

—John 12:1–8

Reflections on extravagant gifts of friendship I have received from others...

_____

_____

_____

_____

_____

_____

_____

_____

_____

_____

_____

_____

_____

A gift opens the way for the giver and ushers him into the presence of the great.

—Proverbs 18:16

Every good and perfect gift is from above, coming down from the Father of the heavenly lights.

—James 1:17

Chapter Five

The Forgiveness of Friendship

$\mathcal{I}$ demonstrated My love for you, sending My Son to die for you while you were still a sinner. There is no condemnation for those who are in Christ Jesus. Through Him, the law of the Spirit of life set you free from the law of sin and death. As far as the east is from the west, I've removed your transgressions from you.

Love Always,

Your God

—from Romans 5:8; 8:1–2; Psalm 103:12

Inspirational
Message

❧

$\mathcal{F}$riends share a special something that is rich, rare, powerful, and persuasive. They offer it without cost to each other, and yet it holds extreme value. If it were a commodity, it would be considered priceless. If it were a precious stone, its value would be immeasurable. If it were a painting, it would be the most coveted of all works of art. What is it? *Forgiveness.* One simple word, phrase, or touch that transforms heartbreak into healing, sadness into celebration, and tragedy into triumph.

Forgiveness from a friend brings restoration and renewal that sends the heart soaring. Forgiveness changes the direction of a friend's steps, alters the plans for the future, and changes the darkness of night into the light of morning.

Don't ever doubt the power of forgiveness, and never believe the lie that friends never let each other down. In fact, friendship may be measured by the weight of the forgiveness granted or received.

Close your eyes and let the shadow of a cross two thousand years old move across your heart and define friendship and forgiveness. Feel its weight as it is lifted off of your shoulders and placed on One who calls you friend. That friend took your nails, your thorns, your spear, and your transgressions and offered you His forgiveness. He did it to show that failures are not fatal and that the soil of friendship raises a harvest of forgiveness.

You may be the friend who needs forgiveness, or you may be the one granting it. You may be the friend who needs to offer it, or the one who needs to ask for it. Either way, go ahead and do what supreme friendship calls you to do with this assurance in your heart: Once forgiveness is given or accepted, no power on earth can dilute the love and loyalty it produces.

You can count on this—the past ended one second ago.

From this point onward,

you can be clean, filled with His Spirit,

and used in many different ways for His honor.

—CHARLES R. SWINDOLL

Falling Back
and
Finding
Forgiveness

As he raised his face toward heaven, he breathed deeply through his long, narrow, sun-baked nose, trying to catch every bit of the salty sea wind blowing over him from the southeast. He had forgotten the strangely alluring fragrance during his past three years of travel. Although the once-familiar smells emanating from the Sea of Galilee should have brought the welcomed comfort of returning home to this northwest shore community, for Peter the disciple, it had the completely opposite effect. The sandy beach he had once fished from for his livelihood held no appeal for him now.

Peter had left this place of his youth and young adulthood three years ago on a mission, and coming back here meant a retreat from that mission—and Peter wasn't the sort who liked to retreat from anything. As he looked wistfully along the shoreline, Peter's thoughts drifted through those three eventful years.

He thought first of that fateful day when, just a few short steps from where he now sat, Jesus had voiced the simple words that would change his path, passion, and purpose. Peter mouthed the words and whispered them faintly to himself. "Come, follow Me," Jesus had said, "and I will make you fishers of men." As the words echoed through his mind, the mixture of the salt air and the voice that hung on the wind on that life-changing day stung his weary heart with sadness and wrung tears from his dark eyes. It had seemed so easy to drop everything and follow this average man with the extraordinary magnetism.

He then turned his gaze out to the sea and squinted as if to pinpoint the place where, at the invitation of his teacher, leader, and most trusted friend, he had actually walked on top of the water. Peter closed his eyes and wiggled his toes as he tried to recapture the astounding sensation of feeling the waves become solid under every step. But his smile quickly gave way to a frown as Peter remembered the embarrassment of falling under the waves after becoming frightened by the wind. He looked longingly at the wrist Jesus had so firmly grasped to rescue him from the angry sea. Peter now whispered, as if speaking to someone close by, "You were always rescuing me from something, weren't You?"

With the words still fresh on his lips, the one memory Peter wanted to forget more than any other rushed into his heart like an unexpected squall. Suddenly Peter imagined himself in a courtyard. Curious onlookers asked him if he was one of the disciples of this Jesus who had just been turned over to the authorities for trial. As he watched the scene unfold in his mind, he heard himself say, "I don't know what you're talking about."

Again he heard the question, and again he heard himself say the horrible words: "I don't know the man." Peter tried to stop the nightmarish scene that ran through his mind, but he couldn't. The final denial came bursting through all his defenses, and he heard the words loud and clear, emphasized with a curse: "I don't know the man!"

The courtyard scene went dramatically silent as he recalled the crowing of a rooster and the lone figure of Jesus standing among His tormentors. Jesus' eyes had locked on to Peter's, and tears had run down His bloodied cheeks.

Peter now stood and looked painfully toward the heavens. Angrily, he beat his chest and shouted toward the now darkening sky, "Why did I forsake You? You were always rescuing me from something, and I couldn't even stand with You in Your time of greatest need." And he fell to the sand and wept as bitterly as he had the night of the denial.

Now, when Peter's friends, Thomas, Nathaniel, James, and John—who were with him on the beach—saw Peter fall to the ground and openly weep, they rushed to see what was wrong. Peter looked up into their concerned faces, stood and hugged each one, and simply said, "I'm going out to fish." In unison, they all replied, "We'll go with you."

Early the next morning, after a frustrating and fruitless night of fishing, a lone figure stood on the beach and called out to them, "Friends," He said, "haven't you caught any fish?"

"No," they answered disgustedly.

The mysterious figure called out again, "Throw your net on the right side of the boat, and you will find some."

When they did, their net became so full of fish that they were unable to haul it in.

John was the first to recognize the man on the shore and said almost in a whisper, "It is the Lord!" Peter squinted his eyes to see if he could verify the words of John, then jumped into the water and swam for shore, riding each wave as far as he could, while the others towed the net full of fish.

When Peter reached the shore, he stopped short of where Jesus stood and looked longingly at Him while panting heavily. Nothing was said between them until Jesus took His outer cloak and wrapped it around Peter, pointed at a fire of burning coals where fish were cooking, and said to all of them, "Bring some of the fish you have caught."

None of them dared ask who He was; for in their hearts, they knew it was the Lord. When they had finished eating, Jesus moved behind Peter, placed His hands on his shoulders, and said, "Simon son of John, do you truly love Me more than these?"

Peter looked at the others one by one, then looked down to the sand and softly said, "Yes, Lord, You know that I love You."

Jesus replied, "Feed My lambs."

Jesus now moved to the right of Peter and knelt down beside him with His hand on his right shoulder and again said, "Simon son of John, do you truly love Me?"

Peter, not wanting to meet the eyes of Jesus, looked off toward the sea and spoke more firmly, "Yes, Lord, You know that I love You."

While rubbing Peter's shoulder, Jesus replied once more, "Take care of My sheep."

Jesus now moved and sat directly in front of Peter, put both hands on his shoulders, looked into Peter's eyes, and slowly and deliberately asked for the third time, "Simon son of John, do you love Me?"

Peter, feeling hurt because Jesus asked him the third time, placed his own hands on the shoulders of Jesus and with tears running from his eyes into his beard said slowly and deliberately, "Lord, You know all things; You know that I love You."

With the three haunting denials of Jesus answered by the three affirmations of Peter's love, Jesus lifted Peter to his feet and said, "Feed My sheep." As Jesus spoke of the future with Peter, He took Peter's hand and led him a few steps from where they were standing. Once more, Jesus placed His hands on the shoulders of Peter and said, "Follow Me!" After embracing Jesus, Peter realized that Jesus had led him to the exact place on the beach where three years earlier he had heard that same voice say those same words. Now assured of his friend's forgiveness, Peter whispered to himself, "Anywhere."

Scriptural Account

"I'm going out to fish," Simon Peter told them, and they said, "We'll go with you." So they went out and got into the boat, but that night they caught nothing.

Early in the morning, Jesus stood on the shore, but the disciples did not realize that it was Jesus.

He called out to them, "Friends, haven't you any fish?"

"No," they answered.

He said, "Throw your net on the right side of the boat and you will find some." When they did, they were unable to haul the net in because of the large number of fish.

Then the disciple whom Jesus loved said to Peter, "It is the Lord!" As soon as Simon Peter heard him say, "It is the Lord," he wrapped his outer garment around him (for he had taken it off) and jumped into the water. The other disciples followed in the boat, towing the net full of fish, for they were not far from shore, about a hundred yards. When they landed, they saw a fire of burning coals there with fish on it, and some bread.

Jesus said to them, "Bring some of the fish you have just caught."

Simon Peter climbed aboard and dragged the net ashore. It was full of large fish, 153, but even with so many the net was not torn. Jesus said to them, "Come and have breakfast." None of the disciples dared ask him, "Who are you?" They knew it was the Lord. Jesus came, took the bread and gave it to them, and did the same with the fish.

When they had finished eating, Jesus said to Simon Peter, "Simon son of John, do you truly love me more than these?"

"Yes, Lord," he said, "you know that I love you."

Jesus said, "Feed my lambs."

Again Jesus said, "Simon son of John, do you truly love me?"

He answered, "Yes, Lord, you know that I love you."

Jesus said, "Take care of my sheep."

The third time he said to him, "Simon son of John, do you love me?"

Peter was hurt because Jesus asked him the third time, "Do you love me?" He said, "Lord, you know all things; you know that I love you."

Jesus said, "Feed my sheep. I tell you the truth, when you were younger you dressed yourself and went where you wanted; but when you are old you will stretch out your hands, and someone else will dress you and lead you where you do not want to go." Jesus said this to indicate the kind of death by which Peter would glorify God. Then he said to him, "Follow me!"

—John 21:3–13, 15–19

Reflections on the role forgiveness has played in a special friendship...

_____

_____

_____

_____

_____

_____

_____

_____

_____

_____

_____

_____

_____

_____

_____

_____

Wounds from a friend can be trusted, but an enemy multiplies kisses.

—Proverbs 27:6

As iron sharpens iron, so one man sharpens another.

— _Proverbs 27:17_

Chapter Six

The Restoration of Friendship

You are accepted in Me! I've redeemed you through My Son's blood and forgiven your sins according to the lavish riches of My all-sufficient grace. Always remember that love has the power to restore and heal. Be kind and compassionate to one another, forgiving each other, just as in Christ I forgave you.

Love,

Your God of Restoration

—from Ephesians 1:6–7; 1 Peter 4:8; Ephesians 4:32

Inspirational
Message

There is an old saying that has been used so frequently that you might easily miss its meaning—but don't. The saying goes like this: "A friend in need is a friend indeed." Whoever coined that phrase spoke volumes about friendship in eight short words.

Where do you turn when you feel crushed by concerns, weary from work, lonely from loss, or stricken by sickness? Who do you picture when you need to see a light at the end of the tunnel, hope at the end of a long road of struggle, or need to feel comfort after enduring a long stretch of sadness? Who comes to mind when you long for understanding and acceptance after you have failed both yourself and others? Who makes you laugh when you feel like weeping or warms your heart when you feel as though you're in a deep freeze? More than likely you would say the name of a person who lives the very words of the saying, "A friend in need is a friend indeed."

Even though you might not know it, your face would be pictured by others who consider you a friend. Friendship brings a rush of responsibility to care, to act, to move, to comfort, to encourage, and to restore. Friends offer outstretched arms to console, a kind touch to soothe, a shoulder to lean on, and an ear to hear.

The best friend the world has ever known said it best, "Come to Me, all you who are weary and burdened, and I will give you rest." Isn't that a true friend? A person who allows you to escape the sadness, struggles, flaws, and failures and simply encourages you to rest.

The world needs friends like you, so keep your arms, eyes, and ears wide open. When you need a friend, don't hesitate to call on one. When you see someone who needs you, don't hesitate to offer the words "Come to me."

After all, a friend in need is a friend indeed.

The most satisfying love

is to be loved in spite of being known.

—Marilyn Meberg

Never Forget the Way Back

"Only a little farther," Josiah said to himself, panting with each labored step. "Only a little farther, and I'll be home." To anyone else, the words and thoughts of home would have brought comfort—but not to Josiah. The thought of home was cloaked with apprehension and shame. He wiped his weathered brow with the filthy sleeve of his outer garment, and for the first time in days, he began to think about his ragged appearance. Feet that had at one time worn the finest footwear were now bare, bleeding, and caked with dirt and mud. He had traded his fine shoes for some measly morsels of bread a few days before. A body that had once been clothed in the finest of silks and woven wool was now covered in apparel made of tattered burlap, fashioned from sacks that had once contained feed for pigs. The elegant clothing had been surrendered to pay off gambling debts months ago. But the greatest embarrassment of all was his hands. Fingers that had been adorned with priceless gold and stones were naked, swollen, scarred, and callous.

It was the first finger of his right hand that caused the most excruciating pain and forced Josiah to his knees, weeping and rocking back and forth while tremors of remorse swept through him. This was the finger that had worn the ring that bore his family seal. It was pure gold, and on the flat surface that surrounded a glistening diamond were the words *Faithfulness and Mercy.* It was now gone, stolen by one of the many "friends" who had disappeared when his money ran out.

Josiah remembered well the day his father, Emmanuel, gave it to him. It was two years ago, on the day before Josiah left home to begin a new life. He was full of hope, dreams, and more money than sense, supplied by his inheritance.

Emmanuel, during a going-away party, had placed the ring on Josiah's finger and, with a prayer of blessing, said, "Almighty God, as I place this ring on Josiah's finger, I ask You to hold him close to Your breast, bless him, and protect him. He is my son, my friend, my right hand, my joy and crown. Never, ever let him forget that true love and friendship will always be found at home." The words had made him burn with anger at the time. Now, they were like flames that licked at his heart and scorched him with sorrow and regret.

Josiah couldn't even remember exactly what had motivated him to leave his father and his brother, Joseph. He did recall some big plans that he and his three friends had discussed when they left for the Decapolis, a city that had grown from ten different communities into one bustling metropolis. But every memory of the preceding two years seemed to blur in an accelerating downward spiral, until a few days ago. That's the day Josiah awoke.

First, his eyes were awakened by the screeching cries from a herd of pigs, among which he was now sleeping. Then, his heart was awakened by a cold realization. He was hungry, and not just for food, but for warmth, acceptance, love, and true friendship. He also realized for the first time that he was dying in every conceivable way a person can die. He was perishing physically, emotionally, and spiritually.

It was there amid the pigs, filth, loneliness, sorrow, and shame that Josiah remembered home and the words his father had prayed, "Never let him forget that true love and friendship will always be found at home." When he came to his senses, he said, "How many of my father's hired men have food to spare, and here I am starving to death! I will set out and go back to my father and say to him: Father, I have sinned against heaven and against you. I am no longer worthy to be called your son; make me like one of your hired men."

Now as he raised his eyes, he saw his home. It sat up on a hill, and under the blazing orange of the setting sun, it glistened like a jewel rising above the golden landscape. Memories flooded his soul. There on that hill to the right of the house, he, Emmanuel, and Joseph had lain together one afternoon, peering up into the sky and describing the different shapes the clouds formed. The huge olive tree to the left was where Emmanuel had taught the brothers to climb and persevere, explaining to them that the view from the top was worth the effort of the climb. Josiah now wondered how he could ever have left such a place, and he said to himself, "Dad, you were right; this is where true love and friendship are found." His pace quickened, and he practiced again what he would say when he faced his father, placing emphasis on the words that expressed his remorse and repentance.

The road crossed a stream where he stopped for a much-needed drink and to wash away the dust from his journey and refresh himself for the coming moments.

As he lowered his head over the water, he saw his reflection for the first time in ages. The face that stared back at him was hideously gaunt and drawn. All signs of youth were gone, replaced by sharp cheekbones, sagging eyes, and harshly weathered skin. In disgust he slapped at the water as if to erase the reflection. All of the anticipation he had felt drained from him in an instant. He arose, looked at his home once more time, and said, "I will not shame you any more than I have." He then turned to walk away.

Suddenly, faintly, he heard his name. "Josiah, Josiah," the voice became louder with every repetition. Josiah turned to see his father with his robe pulled up above his knees, running at full gallop.

Josiah stood motionless, wanting so much to run to Emmanuel but still full of apprehension. Tears poured from his eyes as he realized that his father was both laughing and crying while saying the words, "You're home, Josiah; you're home!" Before Josiah could say anything, Emmanuel threw his arms around him, almost knocking both of them to the ground. Emmanuel kissed Josiah repeatedly, and between each kiss he said, "Josiah, Josiah, you're home!"

Josiah tried to hold him at arm's length so that he could say the words that he had practiced so diligently, "Father, I have sinned against heaven and against you. I am no longer worthy to be called your son."

But Emmanuel smiled and shook his head at Josiah's words. "Do you still not understand, my son?" He then called for his servants, "Quick! Bring the best robe and put it on him, and get some sandals for his feet." Then Emmanuel took his own signet ring, placed it on the first finger of Josiah's right hand, and said, "True love and friendship will always be found at home."

With that, Emmanuel said, "Bring the fattened calf and kill it. Let's have a feast and celebrate. For this son of mine was dead and is alive again; he was lost and is found." So they began to celebrate.

From that day on, it is said, Josiah became the best friend a father ever had.

Scriptural Account

There was a man who had two sons. The younger one said to his father, "Father, give me my share of the estate." So he divided his property between them.

Not long after that, the younger son got together all he had, set off for a distant country and there squandered his wealth in wild living. After he had spent everything, there was a severe famine in that whole country, and he began to be in need. So he went and hired himself out to a citizen of that country, who sent him to his fields to feed pigs. He longed to fill his stomach with the pods that the pigs were eating, but no one gave him anything.

When he came to his senses, he said, "How many of my father's hired men have food to spare, and here I am starving to death! I will set out and go back to my father and say to him: Father, I have sinned against heaven and against you. I am no longer worthy to be called your son; make me like one of your hired men." So he got up and went to his father.

But while he was still a long way off, his father saw him and was filled with compassion for him; he ran to his son, threw his arms around him and kissed him.

The son said to him, "Father, I have sinned against heaven and against you. I am no longer worthy to be called your son."

But the father said to his servants, "Quick! Bring the best robe and put it on him. Put a ring on his finger and sandals on his feet. Bring the fattened calf and kill it. Let's have a feast and celebrate. For this son of mine was dead and is alive again; he was lost and is found." So they began to celebrate.

—Luke 15:11–24

Reflections on a friendship that was damaged and then restored...

_____

_____

_____

_____

_____

_____

_____

_____

_____

_____

_____

_____

_____

When Jesus saw their faith, he said, "Friend, your sins are forgiven."

—Luke 5:20

Chapter Seven

The Faithfulness of Friendship

$\mathscr{B}$e devoted to one another in brotherly love, honoring one another above yourselves. Two are better than one; together, their yield in life is greater than with one alone. For when one of you stumbles or falls, the other one is there to help. A good friend sticks closer than a brother. Remember, all love comes from Me. When you love, you are born of Me and know Me.

Loving You,

$\mathscr{God}$

—from Romans 12:10; Ecclesiastes 4:9–10; Proverbs 18:24; 1 John 4:7

Inspirational
Message

~❧~

Isn't God good? Ever since the beginning, He has seen our need to share our lives in friendship with others. Adam had Eve, Moses had Joshua, and Ruth had Naomi. David depended on Jonathan to save his life, Mary walked with Mary to an empty tomb, and Jesus' close friends shared the intimate moments of His life, His loves, His celebrations, His frustrations, and His final hours.

We are no different, and God knows it. When we fight our daily battles, there are friends to encourage us with their presence. They lie in the foxholes with us, lend us their strength, and march at our sides. When we find ourselves in danger or in trouble, the friends in our lives will not leave us to walk alone—even when it means danger for them.

They stay with us, stride for stride; they warn us of unseen perils and point the way to safety and sanctuary. Friends tell us what we need to hear, hear us when we need to talk, and love us no matter what.

All of this means that you and your friends share wonderful memories that need to be celebrated and shared. These memories shine like diamonds in our past. You and your friends can pick them up, examine each facet, admire the beauty, and enrich the relationship for what is yet to come.

Whatever you do, don't fold up the memories, put them away, and let them gather dust. Break them out often. Let those memories shower your heart with assurance, release your soul with laughter, and bring tears to your eyes.

Friends are friends forever, and so are the rich memories you place in the vault of your heart.

Isn't God good?

A faithful friend is a strong defense;

and he that hath found him

hath found a treasure.

—Louisa May Alcott

Thank You
for the
Memories

As David—the newly appointed King of Israel—walked toward his destination, he should have felt excitement and fulfillment as he remembered the grand coronation he had participated in just the day before. But he felt no satisfaction from the days of elaborate celebration that had heralded his reign as king. In fact, it was this nagging emptiness in his heart that prevented sound sleep and caused him to arise before dawn for his trip to this rather obscure and lonely place.

He was missing someone—someone who should have been there for his long-awaited coronation, but wasn't; someone whose absence was painfully obvious only to David. David alone knew the important role this person had played in helping him reach the throne that he had waited more than fifteen years to fill.

David dreaded his journey's destination because he knew that his arrival would not be greeted with warm embraces, familiar stories of shared memories, or hopeful discussions about the future. No, this visit would simply raise questions about what might have been but never would be. David was visiting a grave site—the place where the body of his finest friend, Jonathan, was buried along with a very large portion of David's heart. David regarded his fallen friend with such reverence that he knew he could not begin his reign as king until he had visited the person whose faith in David's destiny exceeded even his own.

The sun was a bright half circle rising above the horizon when David reached the burial site. Approaching the location of the grave, large tears began to trail down his sun-bronzed cheeks and into his full, dark beard. The last time he had wept was when he had received news of Jonathan's death in battle. He rubbed his midsection and felt himself gasp for air as his stomach began to ache with sorrow. A large stone lay next to the grave site, and David leaned upon it and breathed deeply through his nose to settle his emotions. His muscular arms appeared from under his cloak, and he ran his fingers through his black, shoulder-length hair, pushing it back to allow the fresh sunlight to drench his face. He knelt near the grave and lifted his eyes and hands toward heaven and prayed, "Oh God, how You have poured Your blessings upon Your servant. You have led me to the throne I now possess. You have conquered every one of my enemies, delivered me from every threat, and lifted me to heights I could never have reached on my own. But my heart is filled with sadness because my most trusted friend is fallen and cannot be here to share the day of my deliverance with me. How I ache to see his smile and hear his comforting voice. He believed in Your plans for me even more than I, and I came to trust him like no other."

David wept bitterly as he prayed, and the grief and the morning chill made him shiver. He arose once more and stepped back from the stone, looking at it as if he were seeing it for the first time. Its shape and size aroused a vivid memory of Jonathan. David closed his eyes and let himself visit a morning when he had felt the same kind of chill and sat behind a very similar stone, the stone Ezel, just a little distance from the royal residence of the then-reigning King Saul and his son Jonathan.

David began telling the story to the stone as if he were speaking to Jonathan. "Remember that crisp, cool morning you saved me, Jonathan? It was similar to this morning. The birds were singing wildly, the flowers were in full bloom, and the wind was blowing in the fragrance of the Salt Sea. I remember it as if it were just yesterday. I was standing by the stone Ezel, as you had instructed me to do. I had come to you two days before telling you that your father, the king, was trying to kill me."

David let out a laugh, "I remember your first words after I told you.

"'Never!' you said. 'My father doesn't do anything, great or small, without confiding in me.'

"After I finally convinced you that I was in danger, we came up with a plan. A dinner I was to attend at your father's table was a day away. I would be conspicuously missing, and you would make excuses for me. If Saul reacted violently, you would know that he intended to kill me, and you would come to warn me. If he did not, you would come and tell me I was safe from harm.

"Your signal would be to shoot three arrows near the stone Ezel. If you shouted to the boy with you, 'Look, the arrows are on this side of you,' I was safe. But if you said, 'Look, the arrows are beyond you,' I was in danger. You begged me to trust you, and I did.

"Jonathan, do you remember what you made me promise after we devised our plan? You made me promise that I would remember you and your family, even after every one of my enemies was defeated. Even when I thought I was about to die, you knew God would make me victorious. And you trusted me to remember you.

"I recall waiting at that stone for you, pacing nervously, wondering how I had ever gotten into this mess. Even though the morning was cool, I was sweating heavily. Then I heard your voice tell a little boy to retrieve the arrows you were going to shoot. I hid behind the stone, my heart pounding wildly, as I waited for the signal that would ease my fears or send me away. Then I heard the words that would change my life: 'Isn't the arrow beyond you?' you shouted. And then, as if talking to the boy but really signaling me, you shouted, 'Hurry! Go quickly! Don't stop!'

"Those words ran through me like a spear. I had ached to hear you tell me everything was fine and that I could come home. But your words confirmed my fears, and my heart sank with grief. It wasn't fine, and I wasn't coming home.

"After you sent the boy away, I got up from my hiding place and came to you. Your swollen eyes and pained expression told me all I needed to know. I embraced you and kissed you on the cheek, and we wept together. As I turned to go, you reminded me once more of our sworn friendship before the Lord. Your exact words were, 'The Lord is witness between you and me and between your descendants and my descendants forever.'

"Well, trusted friend, it has happened just as you believed it would. My enemies are gone, and I now sit on the throne of Israel. The only thing that neither of us expected is that you are not with me. But I have not forgotten you and never will. Our sworn friendship will be remembered forever. I trusted you, and you saved me. Now that I am king of Israel, you can trust that your family has nothing to fear. I will care for any of yours as if they were mine."

David leaned against the stone and spoke to the grave for another hour, reminiscing on the past and reporting the details of the coronation. Then David stood and said, "It is time for me to go, my friend; I must be back to my responsibilities before evening." As he walked away from the grave of Jonathan, he turned back one last time and said, "We shall meet again, my friend; trust me."

Scriptural Account

Then David fled from Naioth at Ramah and went to Jonathan and asked, "What have I done? What is my crime? How have I wronged your father, that he is trying to take my life?"

"Never!" Jonathan replied. "You are not going to die! Look, my father doesn't do anything, great or small, without confiding in me. Why would he hide this from me? It's not so!"

But David took an oath and said, "Your father knows very well that I have found favor in your eyes, and he has said to himself, 'Jonathan must not know this or he will be grieved.' Yet as surely as the LORD lives and as you live, there is only a step between me and death."

Jonathan said to David, "Whatever you want me to do, I'll do for you."

So David said, "Look, tomorrow is the New Moon festival, and I am supposed to dine with the king; but let me go and hide in the field until the evening of the day after tomorrow. If your father misses me at all, tell him, 'David earnestly asked my permission to hurry to Bethlehem, his hometown, because an annual sacrifice is being made there for his whole clan.' If he says, 'Very well,' then your servant is safe. But if he loses his temper, you can be sure that he is determined to harm me."

Then Jonathan said to David: "May the LORD be with you as he has been with my father. But show me unfailing kindness like that of the LORD as long as I live, so that I may not be killed, and do not ever cut off your kindness from my family—not even when the LORD has cut off every one of David's enemies from the face of the earth."

So Jonathan made a covenant with the house of David, saying, "May the LORD call David's enemies to account." And Jonathan had David reaffirm his oath out of love for him, because he loved him as he loved himself.

Then Jonathan said to David: "…The day after tomorrow, toward evening, go to the place where you hid when this trouble began, and wait by the stone Ezel. I will shoot three arrows to the side of it, as though I were shooting at a target. Then I will send a boy and say, 'Go, find the arrows.' If I say to him, 'Look, the arrows are on this side of you; bring them here,' then come, because, as surely as the LORD lives, you are safe; there is no danger. But if I say to the boy, 'Look, the arrows are beyond you,' then you must go, because the LORD has sent you away. And about the matter you and I discussed—remember, the LORD is witness between you and me forever."

Then Saul said to his son Jonathan, "Why hasn't the son of Jesse come to the meal, either yesterday or today?"

Jonathan answered, "David earnestly asked me for permission to go to Bethlehem. He said, 'Let me go, because our family is observing a sacrifice in the town and my brother has ordered me to be there. If I have found favor in your eyes, let me get away to see my brothers.' That is why he has not come to the king's table."

Saul's anger flared up at Jonathan and he said to him, "You son of a perverse and rebellious woman! Don't I know that you have sided with the son of Jesse to your own shame and to the shame of the mother who bore you? As long as the son of Jesse lives on this earth, neither you nor your kingdom will be established. Now send and bring him to me, for he must die!"

"Why should he be put to death? What has he done?" Jonathan asked his father.

In the morning Jonathan went out to the field for his meeting with David. He had a small boy with him, and he said to the boy, "Run and find the arrows I shoot." As the boy ran, he shot an arrow beyond him. When the boy came to the place where Jonathan's arrow had fallen, Jonathan called out after him, "Isn't the arrow beyond you?" Then he shouted, "Hurry! Go quickly! Don't stop!" The boy picked up the arrow and returned to his master. (The boy knew nothing of all this; only Jonathan and David knew.) Then Jonathan gave his weapons to the boy and said, "Go, carry them back to town."

After the boy had gone, David got up from the south side of the stone and bowed down before Jonathan three times, with his face to the ground. Then they kissed each other and wept together—but David wept the most.

Jonathan said to David, "Go in peace, for we have sworn friendship with each other in the name of the LORD, *saying, 'The* LORD *is witness between you and me, and between your descendants and my descendants forever.'" Then David left, and Jonathan went back to the town.*

—1 Samuel 20:1–7, 12a, 13b–23, 27b–32, 35–42

Reflections on how the faithfulness of a friend has seen me through difficult times...

_____

_____

_____

_____

_____

_____

_____

_____

_____

_____

_____

_____

I am a friend to all who fear you, to all who follow your precepts.

—Psalm 119:63

My friend shall forever be my friend, and reflect a ray of God to me. — HENRY DAVID THOREAU